FUNDIS

SUNSET'S CLOSE,
TURNS TO REST,
FADING ROSE
FRON WEST.

STARS EMERGE,
ROBE OF NIGHT
VERGE TO VERGE
LS OF LIGHT.

DISTANT HILLS
SEEM AWARE
LDS AND THRILLS
AND NEAR.

FAR
HORIZONS

FAR
HORIZONS

BY
BLISS CARMAN

BOSTON
SMALL, MAYNARD & COMPANY
PUBLISHERS

Printed in the United States of America

THE MURRAY PRINTING COMPANY
CAMBRIDGE, MASS.
THE BOSTON BOOKBINDING COMPANY
CAMBRIDGE, MASS.

To His Honor
WALTER C. NICHOL
Lieutenant Governor of British Columbia
in Happy Remembrance of a Fine
Friendship

MIRALOMA

THERE is a hill on Saanich
And a wild grove thereby,—
I never knew so fair a place
This side of Arcady.

Blue and at peace about it,
The waters of All Bay
As magical as those whereon
The isle of Sappho lay.

In spring the small wood lilies
Go dancing on the breeze,
Where the sun weaves its ancient spell
Among the shadowing trees.

The minstrel air recaptures
The haunting melody
Of sunlit groves and lyric days
By the Sicilian sea,

Where one might find at evening
Pan's hoofprint on the shore,
Or traces where a fleeing nymph
Had passed an hour before;

Where life had time to tarry
Through golden hours all still
Under the green arbutus shade
With Dawn or Daffodil,—

Hearing the songs of Flaccus
With his Falernian wine,
Or Virgil's stately questioning,
So human, so divine.

O beauties of old Hellas
And songs of yesteryear,
Were ever in your Golden Age
Such golden hours as here,—

Today, in Miraloma,
The welcome of a friend,
By peaceful waters of the West.
At Far Horizons' end!

CONTENTS

CONTENTS

FAR
HORIZONS

LORD OF THE FAR HORIZONS

Lord of the far horizons,
Give us the eyes to see
Over the verge of sundown
The beauty that is to be.
Give us the skill to fashion
The task of thy command,
Eager to follow the pattern
We may not understand.

Masters of ancient wisdom
And the lore lost long ago,
Inspire our foolish reason
With faith to seek and know.
When the skein of truth is tangled
And the lead of sense is blind,
Foster the fire to lighten
Our unillumined mind.

Lord of the lilac ranges
That lift on the flawless blue,
Grant us the heart of rapture
The earlier ages knew—
The spirit glad and ungrudging,
And light as the mountain air,
To walk with the Sons of Morning
Through the glory of Earth the fair.

1

A MIRAGE OF THE PLAINS

As I stood on the bank of the river that runs
  by Saskatoon,
I saw the incredible happen in the sober
  light of noon.

I looked out over the prairie as far as the
  eye could see,
And never a stone as big as your hand, and
  never the sign of a tree;
Only the golden stubble with the first light
  snow between,
In the fairy light of a primal world where
  beauty first was seen.

Then far on the dipped horizon where the
  sailing cloud-tops show,
I saw, like a ghost in the sunlight, a prairie
  schooner go.
And after her labored others in a trailing
  caravan—
Lumbering, crude, ill-fitted—but they carried
  the hope of man.

A marvellous train unnumbered, swinging before my gaze,
They passed on into the sundown, and were
  lost in the lilac haze.
I cleared my eyes of the vision—or the
  tremor of sunlit-glare—
Only the golden stubble and the sailing clouds
  were there.

Again I looked to the Northward as far as
the eye could range,
And never a rise nor a foothill, never a hint
of change,
Till a picture rose before me like a mirage
at sea,
Or those wonders of incantation from Indian
jugglery.

And I beheld no longer the voyaging clouds
hull-down,
But towers of beautiful cities and homes of
many a town,
And over them all was gladness and peace
and freedom from care,
And I heard the laughter of children ring on
the frosty air.

And over the whispering snowdrift a far-off
voice said,
"No man shall injure his neighbor, and none
shall make you afraid.
Lo, I am with you always unto the end of
the world."
Then, as the vision faded, the sails of the
clouds were furled.

And there, all round about me, real in the
noonday sun,
Stood Houses of Learning and Beauty—the
vision's fulfillment begun.

ST. GEORGE'S IN THE PINES

St. George that savest England,
Save us who still must go
Where leads thy cross of scarlet
Upon its field of snow!

Beyond the life of cities,
Distractions and dismays,
Where mountain shadows measure
The passing of the days.

Among the lonely snow-peaks
Where golden morning shines,
Stands thy undaunted outpost
Among the lodge-pole pines—

A little stone-built chapel
As modest as can be,
Touched with a loving glory,
To house thy God and thee.

Here, where majestic beauty
And inspiration bide,
Be thou, to make us worthy,
Our counsellor and guide.

Be with us, Soul of England,
Where the last trail puts forth,
To keep unsoiled forever
The honor of the North.

SONG OF THE KICKING HORSE

By Kicking Horse River, through Kicking
    Horse Pass,
Where the Rockies guard their own,
There's a trail that goes by a way it knows
Through valleys wild and lone,—
The trail of the guides and the pioneers
Who passed—a nameless host—
To open the gates for men to come
Down to the Fairy Coast.

By Kicking Horse River, through Kicking
    Horse Pass,
Their wonder trail still leads,
Though little we praise their heroic days
And men have forgotten their deeds.
Are you old or sad or worn or mad,
And sick of life's too great cost?
If you know that way, you will go that way,
To find what you have lost.

By Kicking Horse River, through Kicking
    Horse Pass,
The Road to Tomorrow lies;
And the guides who wait at the sundown gate
Are Fearlessness, Faith, Surmise.
They answer each hail and show the trail
To all men value most.
There is freedom and space and Heaven's
    grace
In the gift of the Magical Coast.

DOWN THE PASS

OVER the rim of the rocky pass
I saw the sage-green moon
Come forth and dance on the silent snow,
Like a girl with silver shoon.

Oh, fairy-work was the spell she wove,
For the trees spun round with her,
As she cast her veil of golden mist
O'er lodge-pole pine and fir.

And ever she sped from hill to hill,
As down the pass we flew,
Till hand in hand, for her saraband,
The hills were whirling too.

In gold and green through each ravine
She led them dumb and fond,
And the sparkling drift would sink and lift
To the lure of her gleaming wand.

For Beauty is ever a sorceress,
And we must dance with her,
Whether we be the children of men
Or the seed of the pine and fir.

DAVID THOMPSON

A GRAY Coat boy from London
At fourteen came over sea
To a lonely post on Hudson's Bay,
To serve the H. B. C.
A seeker of knowledge, a dreamer of dreams,
And a doer of deeds was he.

Before his feet lay a continent
Untrailed, unmapped, unguessed.
The whisper of the mysterious North,
The lure of the unknown West,
Called to him with a siren's voice
That would not let him rest.

'Twas but a step from the factor's door
And the wilderness was there,
Rivers stretching a thousand miles,
Lakes for his thoroughfare,
And forests fresh from the hand of God,
Waiting his will to dare.

Plains that dipped to the edge of the sky
Untracked from rim to rim,
The sorcery when the sun was high
On ranges far and dim,
The summer morns and the winter nights,
They laid their spell on him.

Where did they lead, those waterways?
Where did they end, those plains?
And what is the joy of the wilderness
Only its lover attains?
Ask little Whitethroat, Killooleet,
Who sings through the soft gray rains!

7

Wherever they led, whatever the end,
This lad must find and know.
With pole and paddle and slender birch,
On snowshoes over the snow,
With saddle and pack and pony track,
'Twas his dream and delight to go.

He followed the song the rivers sang
Over their pebbly bars;
By spruce and larch he tallied his march;
The moons were his calendars;
And well he could reckon and read his path
By the faithful shining stars.

From the Churchill to the Assiniboine
And up the Saskatchewan,
Back and forth through all the North
His purpose drove him on,
Making a white man's trail for those
Who should come when he was gone.

So the days grew years, and the years a life,
Without reward or renown,
No heed of self, no greed for pelf
Nor the idle ease of Town,
Till he came at last to the barrier
Where the wheeling sun went down.

There the enormous ranges stood
Forbidding against the sky,
Where only the bear and the bighorn climbed
And the eagle's brood could fly.
His was the foot must find a road
For the world to enter by.

8

Up he followed the azure thread
Of the winding branch for guide,
By rapid and reach and shingly beach,
Then over the great divide.
Then he saw a river broad and strong
Swing past in a silver tide.

Down through a maze of canyon walls
He watched the mighty stream
Sweep on in conquering plenitude
With arrowy flight and gleam,
And knew that he had found at last
The river of his dream.

And here his house was builded.
Here let us stand and say,
Here was a man—full sized—whose fame
Shall never pass away,
While the stars shine and the rivers run
In the land of the Kootenay.

Invermere, B. C.,
August, 1922.

MANACHABAN

Up the Manachaban Valley the white man
    calls the Bow,
When ice lay blue on the ledges and the
    passes were packed with snow,
I went with my brother Assiniboines ages
    and ages ago.

From rock peaks gaunt and crusted the tail-
    ing snow-banners blew,
Like smoke from the pointed tepees in a
    camp of the Manitou.

Snow on the blue-green spruces and the
    tapering lodge-pole pines,
Snow on the gray-green poplars lifting their
    smooth slim lines,

A smother of snow in the heavens where the
    cold white sun shone pale,
And a hand that clung to our snowshoes, as
    we broke the knee-deep trail.

Then down from the North came swirling the
    Warriors of the Sky.
Out of the wild Lost Canyon their level
    charge came by.

The tall pines swayed together moaning as if
    they knew,
While driving in clouds above us the ice-
    barbed arrows flew.

10

We heard them hiss in the willows as they
  sank and settled from flight,
While still the white hosts followed hiding
  the sun from sight.

We gathered our buckskins about us, and
  leaned to the slant of the storm,
And thought of our far-off lodges with their
  fires bright and warm.

Swift as a white owl swooping, the peril
  unlooked-for came,
And fell on that band of hunters,—the shadow
  they feared to name.

Lost! was the sun in the heavens; darker the
  short day grew.
Strange were the passes about us, in a place
  we had thought we knew.

Lost! was the trail behind us. There in the
  formless vast
The track of our snowshoes was buried almost
  before we had passed.

Heavier grew the going, more uncertain the
  light.
And we thought of the Silent Walker, who
  appears at the edge of night,

At the side of the daring traveller with unknown miles to go,
A shadow out of the shadows leaving no
  track in the snow.

The wisest shall not outwit him, nor the
strongest outreach his stride.
And those whom his gray hand touches must
falter and turn aside.

They shall not return to their lodges where
their women and children are,
Nor camp by their own bright rivers that
flow towards the morning star.

They must tarry in that Lost Valley of the
North, which no man knows,
Where the pale Ghost Lights go trailing over
the drifting snows.

And so we fell upon silence and were touched
with cold white sleep,—
The spell of the Shadow Walker, his eerie
way to keep.

The clean snow covered our bodies. The
spring wind bringing the rain
Whispering over the ranges signalled to us
in vain.

The summers returned in their season to
flower the prairie floor,
And Wawa came back to his reed-bed, but
we to our tribe no more.

So did we pass from our hunting and were
lost on that mountain trail,
As the flame dies down to an ash at the
end of a camp-fire tale.

Lost? And forever? Then how is it all so
  familiar today,—
The sifting snow in the willows, the creak
  of the snowshoe's play,

The very bend of the river where Sundance
  Canyon lies,
And the swaying pines in the smother as the
  sun pales out of the skies?

Why should I cry to my senses in this nine-
  teen-twenty-four,
As up the Manachaban Valley we swing to
  the stride once more,
Breasting a glorious snow storm, "I have
  been here before!"

THE PLACE OF VISION

THERE is a Place of Vision,
Where the youth of the Kootenays,
At the approach of Manhood,
Came in the olden days,—

Awaiting the breath of the Spirit,
Alone with the mountains lone,
Each through vigil and fasting
To receive a sign of his own;

A clearing high on a shoulder
Of the lovely Beaverfoot Range
Above the Columbia Valley,
Watching the Seasons change;

A place apart and enchanted,
Surcharged with mystery,—
The breath of things unuttered
And might we cannot see.

There where the wild deer bedded
They trusted the wilderness way.
There with the stars on the ranges
They learned to watch and obey.

Schooled in the deeper knowledge,
Submitting body and will
According to tribal teaching
To a teaching older still,.

With exaltation of spirit
And courageous heart's desire,
Their eager souls were illumined
With a touch of mystic fire.

14

They crossed the threshold of being
Where the cruder senses fail,
And passed the portals of wisdom
That lead to the Shining Trail.

They stood on the verge of creation
In the sweep of the wheeling sun,
In the spell of Magian powers
Where Maker and man are one.

So, even so came the vision
Of the way they must choose and take,
Clear as dawn on the ranges
Bidding the valleys awake.

So, even so came the message,
The law they must learn and keep,
Clear as the wind of morning
Parting the mists of sleep.

Steeped in unnumbered summers
And the peace that has no name,
Lies the place of purified watching
Where the revelation came.

There stands a dead pine guarding
A ring of broken stone.
Lightly we say unheeding,
"The gods have deserted their own!"

Nay, it is we have forgotten
Whence cometh wisdom and might,
Shutting the door on vision,
Turning our backs to the light.

From him who desireth greatly
No wisdom shall be concealed,
To him the future is present,—
All secrets shall be revealed.

In solitude, silence and beauty,
On many a lonely hill
The word on the wind is waiting,
The vision is gleaming still.

THE TRUCE OF THE MANITOU

HERE in the cloudless Northern summer the
    Beaverfoot range lies out in the blue
Brooding and silent, o'er each new-comer its
    old enchantments are cast anew.

He sees in the great plain far below him
    lake and river in silver lie,
The winds from the valley lift to blow him
    chants of the ages passing by.

Voices mysterious wild and haunting speak
    today as they spoke of old,
To the humble in heart and the mind un-
    vaunting is the message brought and the
    secret told.

The Indian lad through lonely hours here
    watched and fasted to prove his worth,
Till there appeared to his quickened powers
    one of the guides of the tribes of earth.

Well he knew that the lower creatures who
    walk or swim or voyage the air,
Whatever their likeness of form or features,
    gull, crow, caribou, seal or bear,

After their kind have each its Master, its
    guiding Spirit, its tribal Soul,
To save from panic and self-disaster, to tem-
    per with reason and self-control.

17

Who drills the ducks in late September, in
    floating line or on whistling wing?
Who bids the slumbering bear remember?
    Who guides the run of the salmon in
    spring?

Who teaches the hawk the wondrous curv-
    ing that builds his spirals against the
    sun?
Who steers the flock of sea-snipe swerving
    to dart and dip and flash as one?

Who but a great and brooding being, taking
    at will the image of man,
Endowed with memory and foreseeing, the
    Thought of God for his feckless clan!

The youth has climbed to his lonely station,
    the rite is performed, the vigil set,
The solemn hours of expectation pass,—never
    one that he will forget.

The sun is gone, and the gold-tipped ranges
    are turned to mauve and purple and
    blue.
The dusk comes on, and twilight changes to
    silence and stars. The word comes
    through.

He sees in the dark between the boulders
    wondering eyes that glow and stare,
The great horned heads and thrusting shoul-
    ders of a herd of moose that are watch-
    ing there.

18

Then a luminous Presence tall and splendid,
   in freedom of beauty and strength of
   days,
Took form and spoke,—as doubt was ended,
   —searching the lad with level gaze:

"Fear not, my son, what lies before thee.   I
   bring thee word from the moose thy kin.
The door of their lodge is open for thee;
   be of good heart and enter in.

"From near and far they are come to know
   thee,—the mightiest bulls of many a
   herd,—
To witness the Manitou's truce and show thee
   they too are bound by the uttered word.

"To these in loyalty and compassion shall
   thy protection and love be shown,
And they in their simple strength and fashion
   shall return thee caring like thine own.

"Little have they of understanding, being but
   folk of the Dawning Mind,
Yet to the Will of the All-commanding in
   goodness of heart they are not blind.

"Toward them thou shalt brook no hurt nor
   treason; they are thy brothers from this
   day forth.
With them thou shalt share the Lesser Reason
   and be given the Knowledge of all the
   North.

19

"I will be with thee in all thy goings, wak-
ing or sleeping by day or night,
With the rain on its march and the wind in
its blowings. Thy kinsman the moose
will lend thee might.

"Thou shalt have eyes where others see not,
a heart for the trail where others faint.
Ill-willed nor wanton thou shalt be not, keeping thy senses clean of taint.

"In thine hour of peril when none is near
thee, when evil threatens and help is far,
Call on thy brothers and they shall hear thee
and aid on the instant wherever they are.

"The Darkness has lightened. The Silence
has spoken. Go, and forget not and be
strong."
The vision faded, the spell was broken. And
the youth who had pondered long and
long

Arose and went down where the valley waited
and the thin blue morning smoke up-
curled
From the silent lodges, with heart elated; a
splendor lay over all his world.

WORD FROM THE MOCCASIN TRAIL

FROM the land of the Abanakis,—
The rivers and hills of the East,—
An Indian spirit sends greeting
To the great Trail Riders' feast.

Afoot and alone with peril
We went with arrow and bow.
Mounted, unarmed and jesting,
In safety at ease you go.

Little enough was our learning,
Small was our craft and skill.
But we saw the feet of the morning
Go by,—and our hearts were still.

We shaped the canoe and the paddle,
We fashioned the snowshoe frame,
And the Great Spirit was with us,
As we kindled the council flame.

You have circled the earth with your
        knowledge,
Your magic is more and more.
Yet must you heed our wisdom,—
The truth of the wilderness lore.

You ride to make good our beginnings,
Our trails to keep clear and extend,
Guarding the lodge and the camp fire,
In peace at sundown's end.

So over all we are tribesmen,
By the law that does not swerve,—
At home in the Tent of the Open,
On call through the Great Reserve.

We lift you the friendly signal,
We send you our sign on the air.
Look East for our smoke at evening.
And say, "Our brothers are there!"

"May no foot want for a stirrup,
No prayer nor adventure fail,
And the Master Guide go with you,"
Is the word from the Moccasin Trail.

Moonshine,
Twilight Park,
In the Catskills,
July, 1924.

TRAVELLER'S JOY

By the pass of the Coquahalla,
Where the roadbed snakes and clings
To the soaring perilous rockface—
Where an eagle needs his wings;

Down through the wooded canyons
Of the Otter and Tulameen,
Where first October wanders
Pale gold through the sombre green;

You will come to the Okanagan,
And meet a breath of the South,
Where the wind that brings fair weather
Comes up from the valley's mouth.

You may ride to the gates of morning
On slopes of yellow pine
And flats of sage and greasewood,
In a country I call mine.

You may camp in the open timber
On the level-floored plateaus,
When sunset dyes the tree trunks
Cinnamon, purple and rose,

While blued in the smoke of evening
The pink-gray ranges rise,—
With the piney smell in your nostrils,
And your heart in Paradise.

MATERIA MEDICA

WHAT are these unknown flowers
That star this lovely earth
Wasting through long sweet hours
Their beauty and their worth?

What are these plants unknown
That paint the desert's floor
With a splendor all their own,
Unheeded o'er and o'er.

O foolish Man and blind,
Here is Earth's healing grace
For thee and all thy kind
To build the perfect race.

There springs no smallest flower
In all the wilderness
But God has given it power
To lighten some distress.

Their truth shall make thee wise,
Their virtues make thee whole,
Their glory fill thine eyes
With loveliness of soul.

This earth is holy ground,
And every seed and spore
In verity is bound
Life's harmony to restore.

Each with its balm for pain
Shall serve thy need, and prove
They take God's name in vain
Who reckon without love.

IN THE OKANAGAN

I HEAR the sweet larks crying.
The soft wind in the pines
Is like a great sea sighing
For what its heart divines.
The hills stand up in splendor;
The dark blue shadows lean
Against them deep and tender;
The far-blown air is clean.

From Skaha to Osoyoos
The temperate days go by
With simple life and joyous
Under a stainless sky.
The gray unbroken benches
Are crowned with yellow sage,
And ageless beauty quenches
The fever of our age.

Here balsam poplars capture
The scent of Paradise,
And strange new flowers enrapture
Our unaccustomed eyes.
The trees with fruit are bending,
The gardens gay with flowers,
A sense of peace unending
Is over all the hours.

Along the purple ranges
The glow of sunset shines,
And glory spreads and changes
Among the red-boled pines.
Here time takes on new leisure
And life attains new worth.
And wise are they who treasure
This Eden of the North.

KALEEDEN ROAD

THERE is a road by Skaha Lake
The cautious driver will not take,
So narrow, steep and high in air—
And dangerous as an open stair—
He turns aside to easier grades
Through stands of pine in crimson glades.

But you who would behold the face
Of Beauty in her dwelling-place,
And know that she is often found
Within a peril-guarded ground,
Loving the fearless, who have shown
A spirit steadfast as her own,

Take the Kaleeden road and dare
The danger for the glory there.
Beauty will meet you as you fly
Enraptured between earth and sky,
And her own ecstasy impart
As guerdon to your faithful heart.

The spell of her enchanted ways
Shall be about you all your days
With the old thrill, as you recall
The loveliness that held you thrall,
And bless the stars that bade you take
Kaleeden road by Skaha Lake.

VANCOUVER

WHERE the long steel roads run out and stop,
And the panting engines come to rest,
Where the streets go down to the arms of the
   sea,
Stands the metropolis of the West.

There the adventurous ships come in
With spices and silks of the East in hold,
And coastwise liners down from the North
With cargoes of furs and gold.

Traders up from the coral isles
With tales of those lotus-eating lands,
And smiling men from the Orient
With idols of jade in their hands.

Yellow and red and white and brown,
With stories in many an outland tongue,
They mingle and jest in her welcoming streets,
As they did when Troy was young.

The sceptre passes and glory fades,
Only the things of the heart stand sure.
Fame and fortune are blown away,
Friendship and love endure.

Here is friendship steady of hand,
Loving-kindness fearless and free—
Men and women who understand,
And romance as old as the sea.

Tyre and Sidon, where are they?
Where is the trade of Carthage now?
Here is Vancouver on English Bay,
With tomorrow's light on her brow!

VICTORIA

WHERE the traveller looks from Saanich,
Fair is the sight he sees,
A gracious imperial city
Guarding the gates of the seas,
With a robe of golden English broom
Spreading about her knees.

Lovely, with old-world leisure
Gracing her modest state,
In youthful pride of dominion
She sits by the Western gate,
Watching the liners come and go
Through Juan de Fuca Strait.

She is crowned with ivy and laurel
Fresh with an ageless spring;
Tales of the East and news of the North
Her sheltered sea-lanes bring;
And all her beauteous days go by,
Soft as a gray gull's wing.

Child of the strong adventure,
Bred to the clean and fine,
With touch of the velvet tropics
And eyes with the Northern shine,
Never to be forgotten—
Last of the Sea-Kings' line.

MALAHAT

As we went up on Malahat,
The green hill-road on Malahat,
The foaming river ran beside,
As if in haste to tell the tide
The latest news of Malahat.

Too young to wait, too glad to stay,
Where giant firs met overhead,
Through the dark aisles it flashed and sped
In silver mist with flying spray
Along the way to Malahat.

As on we went through shade and gleam,
We raised the gray-winged gulls from rest
In eddies on the river's breast,
Ice-blue and clear as ocean stream—
Safe in the heart of Malahat.

There, as we mounted, fjord and hill
Unrolled, with wooded isles between,
A paradise in blue and green
That made the amazed heart stand still
Beneath the spell of Malahat.

Far-off, beyond the last sea-line,
Lo, like a floating cloud of rose,
One peak in its eternal snows,
The high-heart's everlasting sign—
A glimpse of heaven from Malahat.

RIVERS OF CANADA

O ALL the little rivers that run to Hudson's
    Bay,
They call me and call me to follow them away.

Missinaibi, Abitibi, Little Current—where they
    run
Dancing and sparkling I see them in the sun.

I hear the brawling rapid, the thunder of the
    fall,
And when I think upon them I cannot stay at
    all.

At the far end of the carry, where the wilder-
    ness begins,
Set me down with my canoe-load—and for-
    giveness of my sins.

O all the mighty rivers beneath the Polar
    Star,
They call me and call me to follow them afar.

Peace and Athabasca and Coppermine and
    Slave,
And Yukon and Mackenzie—the highroads of
    the brave.

Saskatchewan, Assiniboine, the Bow and the
    Qu'Appelle,
And many a prairie river whose name is like
    a spell.

They rumor through the twilight at the edge
    of the unknown,
"There's a message waiting for you, and a
    kingdom all your own.

"The wilderness shall feed you, her gleam
    shall be your guide.
Come out from desolations, our path of hope
    is wide."

O all the headlong rivers that hurry to the
    West,
They call me and lure me with the joy of
    their unrest.

Columbia and Fraser and Bear and Kootenay,
I love their fearless reaches where winds un-
    tarnished play—

The rush of glacial water across the pebbly
    bar
To polished pools of azure where the hidden
    boulders are.

Just there, with heaven smiling, any morning
    I would be,
Where all the silver rivers go racing to the
    sea.

O well remembered rivers that sing of long
    ago,
A-journeying through summer or dreaming
    under snow.

Among their meadow islands through placid
    days they glide,
And where the peaceful orchards are diked
    against the tide.

Tobique and Madawaska and shining Gasper-
    eaux,
St. Croix and Nashwaak and St. John whose
    haunts I used to know.

And all the pleasant rivers that seek the
    Fundy foam,
They call me and call me to follow them
    home.

MANZANITAS

FROM the majesty and mystery and might of
    all the North
In its silence and its honor and its pride,
When south again you turn,
You are like enough to learn
This world is very long as well as wide.

When you meet the Sacramento in the cop-
    per-colored hills,
Its Iron Canyon washed in morning gold,
What perhaps you did not know
May strike you like a blow,—
This world is very new as well as old.

There is mystery in cedar, there is music in
    the pine,
There is magic where the scarlet maples run.
But as strange a spell will hold you
All unreasoned and enfold you
From the blue-green manzanitas in the sun.

The apple trees of Grand Pré and the orchards
    of the North
May charm you where the tide of Fundy spills,
Yet another magic takes you
When another morning wakes you,
Where the manzanitas dot their barren hills.

When you sight the open valley where the
    palms and oaks begin
And snowy Lassen rises from the plain,
There is something in your heart
That will make it stop and start,
At the sight of manzanitas once again.

They will sing you songs of passes where the
      high Sierras lift,
They will tell you old-time stories of the trail.
No day will be too long
As you listen to their song,
And find a new enchantment in each tale.

There is rapture waiting for you at the rim
      of all the world,
There is medicine no pharmacy distills,
There is all of time before you
And only heaven o'er you,
Where the manzanitas call you to the hills.

You shall see the desert sunrise, and the skies
      of turquoise blue
On mountains made of lavender and rose,
And the fever of the quest
Shall be quieted to rest
In a spaciousness that only freedom knows.

You shall watch the starry splendor from a
      blanket on the ground,
The hosts of glory marching by your fire,
And the stillness and the vast
Will reveal to you at last
How simple in the end is soul's desire.

THE MOON SYMBOL

THIS is the sign of the moon
Worn by the tribes of the West,
The sacred symbol of Night
Guarding the love in the breast.

This is the mystical charm
Out of soft moon-metal wrought,
With all of its magic intact,
The Navajo silversmith caught,

When he beheld in the dusk
That marvellous sickle of light
Hang o'er the desert to guide
The footsteps of lovers aright.

Was not a sorcerer here
Casting a silvery spell,
Calling the Manitou down
In the wrought symbol to dwell?

Surely a poet was he,
Seeking a word of his own
For the enchantment of night
He too had seen and known!

Bidding the silver assume
The language of beauty, and be
Witness of love for the dumb
Yet impassioned—even as he.

He too a lover had been,
(Does not his handicraft say?)
Touched with the glamour of life,
And giving his heart away.

See where the hammer-marks prove
The faith of the artist sublime—
Love and its work must abide,
Outlasting the sand storms of time.

Yours be this talisman too,
Lovers of beauty and light,
Leaving your hearts to the care
Of the great spirit of night!

THE THUNDER BIRD

WHAT of our Lord of the sky,
Whose mighty pinion
Over the void of the blue
Swept in dominion?

When the slow beat of his wings
Rustled with thunder,
All the tribes knew it and stood
Spellbound in wonder.

Far in the canyon of day
Was his rock-dwelling,
When he would go or return
Was no foretelling.

Trackless untamed and aloof
Dwelt the Far-seeing,
Giver of life-giving rain,
Quick death decreeing.

Then came the greedy of heart,
The white destroyer,
Casting his noose in the air,—
Reckless decoyer.

Taking the god in a trap,
Taming his power,
Harnessed and broken to toil,
Sold by the hour.

What of the Lord of the storm,—
The desert's vastness,—
Once we revered in our hearts,
Safe in his fastness?

See where the palefaces still
Cower in panic,
Knowing their master at bay,
Instant, titanic,

When, dealing beauty and death,
From the crossed wire
Crashes the god over all—
Thunder and fire.

TECUMSEH AND THE EAGLES

I

TECUMSEH of the Shawnees
He dreamed a noble dream,—
A league to hold their freedom old
And make their peace supreme.
He drew the tribes together
And bound them to maintain
Their sacred pact to stand and act
For common good and gain.

II

The eagles taught Tecumseh
The secret of their clan,—
A way to keep o'er plain and steep
The liberty of Man.
The champions of freedom
They may not weary soon,
Nor lay aside in foolish pride
The vigilance of noon.

Those teachers of Tecumseh
Were up to meet the dawn,
To scan the light and hold the height
Till the last light was gone.
Like specks upon the azure,
Their guards patrolled the sky,
To mount and plane and soar again
And give the warning cry.

They watched for lurking perils,
The death that skulks and crawls,
To take by stealth their only wealth
On wind-swept mountain walls.
They did not trust the shadows
That sleep upon the hill;
Where menace hid, where cunning slid,
They struck—and struck to kill.

Through lonely space unmeasured
They laid their sentry rings,
Till every brood in eyrie rude
Was shadowed by their wings.
Tecumseh watched the eagles
In summer o'er the plain,
And learned their cry, "If freedom die,
Ye will have lived in vain."

III

The vision of Tecumseh
It could not long endure;
He lacked the might to back the right
And make his purpose sure.
Tecumseh and his people
Are gone; they could not hold
Their league for good; their brotherhood
Is but a tale that's told.

IV

The eagles of Tecumseh
Still hold their lofty flight,
And guard their own on outposts lone,
Across the fields of light.

40

They hold their valiant instinct
And know their right of birth,
They do not cede their pride of breed
For things of little worth.

They see on earth below them,
Where time is but a breath,
Another race brought face to face
With liberty or death.
Above a thousand cities
A new day is unfurled,
And still on high those watchers cry
Their challenge o'er the world.

Where patriots are marching
And battle flags are borne,
To South and North their cry goes forth
To rally and to warn.
From border unto border,
They wheel and cry again
That master cry, "If freedom die,
Ye will have lived in vain!"

THE RETURN OF THE MAYFLOWER

I

Down the sparkling Channel,
Out of Plymouth Sound,
What gallant little craft is this
Making outward bound?

Who crowd along her taffrail
To look their last on home,
While the seas beneath her forefoot
Are trampled into foam,

And in the morning sunlight
Her last sail is unfurled?
She's the *Mayflower* out from Plymouth,
Bound for the New World.

What cargo does she carry,
And what port will she make?
She has a hundred souls on board
Would die for conscience' sake.

And she will come to anchor
On a far Western beach,
By God's grace, past the farthest bounds
That tyranny can reach.

No Argo ever carried,
No pilgrim ever planned,
A more sublime adventure
Than this exalted band.

They bear the flower of England,
To plant it over sea—
The holy seed of Runnymede
That men call Liberty.

And lo, that magic blossom
Shall flourish and increase,
To glad the souls of all mankind,
And fill the world with peace.

Warm are the Devon moorlands
In the September sun,
And over the dim unknown sea-rim
The *Mayflower* has gone.

II

Looming up the Channel,
Making Plymouth Sound,
What man-of-war is this that comes
Racing, victory bound?

Speeding as to battle,
On she comes amain,
Swift as an eagle's shadow
Across the summer plain.

In power and in beauty
Commanding on the seas,
She leads a stranger battle line—
What men, what ships are these?

Look, where she flies her colors—
The white and crimson bars,
The ensign of the Rights of Man,
The Glory of the Stars!

Back from the ports of promise
Beyond the Western sea,
These are the breed of Runnymede,
The Sons of Liberty.

To cheers that give her welcome
What answer will she make?
Hark to her thousand souls on board
Would die for freedom's sake!

To stay the ancient altars,
Where fire of justice burns,
For freedom still as God may will,
The *Mayflower* returns.

THE GREEN SCARAB

THIS ring, of course, takes your eye,—
A splendid great scarab of green.
Imagine how Pharaoh went by,
And this on his finger was seen!

Singing girls going before,
Lifting their pæans of praise;
Suppliants bowed to the floor,
Proclaiming his greatness of days;

Fan-bearers following after,
With clash of the cymbals and drums;
Incense that floats to the rafter;
The cry of the flutes where he comes;

Priests in their purple and scarlet,
Dancers in brassiers of gold,
The merchant, the scribe, and the harlot,
The soothsayers shaven and old;

All these are now dust of the East,—
Their vanity, power, and pride
Gone with the flowers of their feast,
Past with their music that died.

And still this symbol remains
A treasure the ages hold fast,—
Sign that the spirit attains
Its mystic perfection at last.

. . . . . .

Guarding the emblem they hold,
How freshly these irises blend,
Wrought in a setting of gold
Designed by George Marcus, my friend!

BELLS OF YS

ONCE of old there stood a beauteous city
By the Breton sea,
Towered and belled and flagged and wreathed
    and pennoned
For the pomp of Yule-tide revelry;
All its folk, adventurous, sea-daring,
Gay as gay could be.

And at night when window, torch, and bon-
    fire
Lighted up the sky,
Down the wind came galleon and pinnace,
Steered for that red lantern, riding high;
Every brown hand hard upon the tiller,
Shoreward every eye.

Well I see that hardy Breton sailor
With the bearded lip,—
How he laughed out, holding his black racer
Where the travelling sea-hills climb and slip,
Chased by storm, but lighted on to haven,
Ship by homing ship.

Every sail came in, a deep-sea rover
Who had heard afar
Wild and splendid hyperborean rumors
Of a respite made to feud and war,—
Making port where sea-wreck and disaster
Should not vex them more.

What of Ys? Where was it when gray
    morning
Gloomed o'er Brittany?
Smothered out in elemental fury,
Wrecked and whelmed in the engulfing sea,
To become a never-fading story
In sea-legendry.

There at ebb of tide, when no wind vexes
That lone tragic shore,
Through the sea's pale light entrancèd towers
May be seen uprising from its floor,
Safe within that beryl deep embosomed
Lovely as of yore.

Still along that haunted coast men tell us
They can hear at times,
When the tide is half asleep and musing,
The faint sound of unsubstantial chimes
Ringing through the world's tumultuous day-
    beat
From enchanted climes.

And they say those peals of fairy music
Are the city's bells,
Drowned long since with all their silver joy-
    ance,—
That a deathless rapture in them dwells,
Part forever of the surge of being
As it sinks and swells.

In each heart there is a sunken city,
Wonderful as Ys.
In hours of ebb we hear the mellow pealing
Of its mystic bells of joy and peace,
Rocked by tides that wash through all its
    portals
Without let or cease.

In from nowhere blow those freshening sea-
    turns,
Haunting all our ways
With melodious inspiring echoes
Of old transports and forgotten days.
Through the entries and the doors of being
Their faint music strays.

That's the magic of our deathless sea-bells,
Chiming all life long
Ever-healing canticles of beauty,
Joy's ecstatic triumph over wrong,—
The love theme that haunts this human dwell-
    ing
With immortal song.

THE GOOD PRIEST OF GOURIN

In dark old Brittany linger
Traditions and tales of the past,
When belief was more moving than now
And the world more wondrous and vast.

Here is a strange sweet legend
That has many a time been told,
But never before was written down
In language new or old.

Passing from lip to lip
Through that province by the sea,
The faith-worn treasure came at last
To the friend who gave it to me.

In the ancient graveyard at Gourin
My friend espied one stone
Quite new, on top of its pediments
Age-worn and lichen-grown.

The old old slab, they said,
As a questioning look they caught,
Was worn away by the feet
Of little children, brought

By mothers to walk on the tomb.
A word of amazement led
To this tale of the ancient days
And the goodness of one long dead.

Hundreds of years ago
In the parish there lived a priest
Greatly beloved by his people
And his children—not the least.

For he loved the little folk
Even as the Master had done
When He took them up in his arms
And blessed them every one.

But one sad human weakness
Afflicted this good curé.
When he had fallen asleep
After his work of the day,

He could hardly be roused again,
But would drift back into sleep,
As a vessel cut from her moorings
Will drift out onto the deep.

One night as he slept there came
A hurried knock at his door,
To summon him to baptize
A little one stricken sore.

Yes, yes, he would come at once!
But frail is our flesh. The tide
Of sleep engulfed him again,
And by morning the child had died.

Grief for the loss of a soul
And remorse tore at his heart.
Unworthy one! He could serve
No longer, he must depart!

So one night, turning his back
On the parish he loved, he set out
For the nearest port, his step
Heavy enough no doubt.

Thence he took ship and sailed
For Ireland, setting his face
To a new life that should repair
His sorry fault, by God's grace.

Nearing the coast, he found
Among his belongings the key—
Thrust in his pocket in haste—
To the door of his Sacristy.

Overboard it must go!
Not a single tie must remain
With all he had loved and lost,
To bring it to mind again.

For years in a new-found home
With patience and love as of old
He labored among the poor
And the suffering in his fold.

And always his chiefest joy
Were the children in his care,
For he loved them tenderly—
That spirit devoted and rare.

And they all loved him till he seemed
Almost a saint in their eyes,
With a touch of glory his worn
Old cassock could not disguise.

So it went, till he stopped on a day
At an inn to sup and eat,
When they set before him a fish
Fresh from the sea for a treat.

As ever before a meal
His thanks to God gave he.
Then lo, inside of the fish—
The key of his Sacristy!

A miracle truly.   But why?
Could it be a mercy shown
To one who had grievously sinned,
Repented, and tried to atone?

How else interpret the marvel?
Rejoicing he read it so,—
The days of his penance were past,
He might arise and go,

Back to the Bretons he loved,
Be with his own once more.
Oh how they welcomed him,
How the children ran from each door!

And there he toiled to his age,
In the footsteps of his Lord
With mercy and healing and love,
And passed to his reward.

He died, but surely his soul
Lives on somewhere, somehow.
See how his tomb is worn
By children's feet even now,

Where mothers bring them to walk
Back and forth on the stone,
To strengthen the frail little bodies!
And he blesses them spirit and bone.

This is the ancient legend
From Gourin among the hills,
Where the faithful still believe,
And all is as God wills.

THE QUEEN OF THE ANGELS

Her church is on the Plaza
Of the old Spanish town,
Where swarthy men and women
In the noon go up and down.

Day long and year long
The palm-tree shadows fall
With the slow-creeping sunlight
On the yellow plaster wall.

Day long and year long
The weathered doors are wide,
That the broken may find healing
And the wayworn turn aside.

For the lonely and distraught ones
There is sanctuary here,
There is pity in the stillness,
And compassion for a tear.

Young lovers find her altar
Where many candles burn,
And breathe their hopes before her
And bare their hearts that yearn.

They look upon their Lady,
And poor is her attire,
But her eyes are like the lilac
For the pain of their desire.

A heavy dull offender,
Laden with miseries,
Up the long aisle in penance
Goes meekly on her knees.

No suppliant too lowly,
No sinner too afraid.
Our Lady of the Angels
Is merciful to aid.

She lifts a hand to bless them,
Forgiving sin and shame;
She is acquaint with sorrow,
And Mary is her name.

THE BROTHERS OF SAINT FRANCIS

THE age of ruthless speeding
Tears madly on today,
But the Brothers of St. Francis
Must fare afoot alway.

No privilege of leisure
Their ministry commands,
With a message in their girdle
For the freeing of the lands.

Yet thrushes fill their twilights
And stars of morning sing,
As they take the dust of travel
On the Business of the King.

Soft sleep and easy faring
For those to riches bound;
For the Brothers of St. Francis
A blanket on the ground.

But ah, what dreams attend them
Before the stars grow wan,—
Visions of joy triumphant
When violence is gone!

The greedy will be fighting
With tooth and nail and sword,
But the Brothers of St. Francis
Must pattern by their Lord.

The foolish will be striving
With words and words and words,
But the Brothers of St. Francis
Have secrets with the birds.

At evening and at morning
They hear their brothers sing,
And their hearts leap up with gladness
On the Highroad of the King.

ST. FRANCIS AND THE BIRDS

St. Francis preached a sermon once,
Not to dominie nor dunce,
Prince nor pauper,—to the birds
He addressed his loving words.

Flocking in from far and near
One and all kept still to hear,
Robin, vireo, and wren
Sitting mute like decent men;

Tanager in scarlet coat,
Golden-wing and ruby-throat,
Bobolink and chickadee,
Like children good as good could be.

From the catbird not a squawk,
Not a whistle from the hawk,
From the raven not a croak;
Not a parrot cracked a joke.

Even the outrageous jay
Sat without a word to say,
And the oriole and thrush
Forced their golden throats to hush.

Grosbeak, meadow-lark, and quail
Let their sliding woodnotes fail,
While the lonely whippoorwill
Ceased his grieving from the hill.

And the whitethroat from the wild
With his music undefiled,
Even he put singing by
For the greater mystery,—

Some new phrase of being's lore
He had never heard before,
Which might turn his plaintive fall
Into triumph after all.

There they waited all intent
For the word the Lord had sent,
Hearing good St. Francis tell
How life's song of joy befell;

How they each must bear a part
In the chorus of the heart,
Keeping harmony alive,
Helping rapture to survive;

For if any voice were dumb
Their Lord's Kingdom could not come,
And the world must pass away
In a wreck at Judgment Day.

As he finished every tree
Sounded like the Litany
When the people make response.
For the bird folk all at once,

With new reason to be glad
Such as they had never had,
Lifted up with one accord
Heart and voice to praise the Lord.

THE PREACHER

See here! This is it!
See here! This is it!

The voice of the preacher all day long
Reiterating his summer song.

In the morning air in the fresh green wood
He seems to argue that life is good.

To follow the trail from day to day
In wisdom and love is the only way.

Preacher, I do believe it's true.
I'll be converted and live like you,

With not a thing in the world to do
But sit in the sun the whole day through,

And be my followers many or few
Preach the gospel according to you.

See here! This is it!
See here! This is it!

MY TEACHERS

THE people of the forest
In crimson, green, and tan,—
The trees,—have been my teachers
To make of me a man.

They awed me with their beauty,
Their tender strength and pride.
They gladden me as comrades
Forever at my side.

I dare not scorn their patience
In learning how to grow.
They do not waste their powers
In rushing to and fro,

Nor spend a moment thinking
How soon they have to die,—
All occupied enhancing
The hour going by.

I love the dark-hued spruces
Because their hearts are warm.
And the tall pines have taught me
To front the winter storm.

Among the April willows
In their gold and silver gear,
I hear the bees make music
And summer drawing near.

Remembered Birch and Lilac
Have taught me loveliness,
They are so fair and fragrant
In their soft-colored dress.

Great Oak, dear Beech and Cedar,
Young Cherry dressed in white,
They stand with heads uncovered
To greet the morning light.

And little trembling Aspen
Who always says her prayers,
Has taught me by example
To tell God all my cares.

And One in gown of scarlet,
The first beloved of all,
Still tells me tales of glory
When autumn days befall.

LADY'S SLIPPER

Who passed this way and left this trace
Of beauty in so wild a place,

To stir our souls with marvelling
At so incredible a thing?

Who sent this living miracle
In the deep Northern woods to dwell,

Where only hermit thrushes come
And the shy brown bear makes his home?

Whence was the inspiration caught?
Whose was the sudden happy thought?

Or whose the impulse thus to bless
The rough untrodden wilderness?

Deep in our hearts glad tidings say,
Beauty herself came by this way,

And with a wisdom older far
Than alphabet or calendar,

Cast off her sandal as she sped
Lest we should miss the way she fled.

And so forever we pursue
The shadowy trail of Beauty's shoe,

And for her sake must leave behind
Riches and rest and peace of mind,

To follow on that shining trace,
With beating heart and breathless pace.

By darkling wood and haunted stream,
Still lured by the enchanting gleam,

Wherever the long way may lead,
To keep the trail is all our need.

On simple fare, in poor attire,
Torn and waylaid by flint and briar,

With the lone dawn upon the height
Or the great desert stars by night,

Through burning sun and blinding snow
Untiring and content we go,

If only so we may behold
Dear Beauty's self ere we are old.

TWILIGHT IN EDEN

In the cool of the day in Eden
There was a Voice that came,
And a Presence walked in the shadows
Calling Adam by name.

In the deep woods at twilight
There is a voice I hear
Haunting the dusk with a burden
Serene and marvellous clear.

Sometimes I think it a seraph,
Sometimes I know 'tis a bird,
And many a time I wonder
If that is what Adam heard.

Lost long since was the secret.
Now no man knows the tongue
Wherein God spake unto Adam
In the days when earth was young.

The light of knowledge is darkened
By panic and greed and pride.
Greatly the Serpent promised,
Greatly indeed he lied.

We have weighed the sun in a balance,
We have ridden the wind in speed,
Vast are our cunning inventions,
But who hath wisdom at need?

We are housed and pampered like princes,
We are clothed with the raiment of kings,
But how shall the soul in her longing
Profit by all these things?

We have scorned the belief of our fathers
And cast their quiet aside,
To take the mob for our ruler
And the voice of the mob for our guide.

You may search the rocks for their record,
You may winnow the stars for a clue,
But where is the rapture of instinct
The morning in Eden knew?

Who can interpret the meaning
Of the wind among the trees,
The warnings of birds and of insects,
Or the rain's soft litanies?

God still walks through the twilight
Waiting for us to hear.
Have we not found His footprint
In the meadows when spring drew near?

Have we not seen His pageant
Autumn in scarlet and gold?
But who stands in awe at His passing?
Who kneels while the message is told?

We have polluted the silence.
How should we hear the voice?
We have discarded reverence,
And made disillusion our choice.

Anarch destroyers of Eden,
Rioting over the lands,—
Room for the smiling witness
Who hearkens and understands!

THE VOICE IN THE GARDEN

PACING my garden rounds with pensive tread
    and slow,
Thinking on those far bounds to all our sight
    can know,—
Sifting as in debate the endless How and Why
Of man's mysterious fate and the soul's bitter
    cry,—

"If one could find," I thought, "a door in that
    blue wall,
Wherethrough there might be caught a glimpse
    for one and all!"
"My son,"—I heard a voice,—"now and for-
    evermore
Thou hast the gift of choice. For thee thy
    chosen door
But needs thine utmost power, to open and
    disclose
Beyond the clouds of thought the glory of
    thine hour.

"O heart of little trust, why falter or despair,
When beauty from the dust is lifted like a
    prayer—
Transcending space and time, outreaching
    sense and thought,
That excellence sublime which cannot come
    to naught!

"No leaf from verge to verge in all the
spring's green sea
But feels the lifting urge of power that sets
it free.
No drop of shining dew that holds the colored
ray,
But it is sphered as true as the great arch of
day.

"Through every bud and blade an ageless
ardor runs,
An equal law is laid on whirling dusts and
suns.
No fernleaf is uncurled, no budsheath breaks
the mould,
But He who made the world sustains it as of
old.

"See, where the budding vine puts forth its
strength at need,
The mystic and divine symbol of life indeed!
Hill-wind and springing grain, brook-song
and evening star,
Hoar frost and summer rain,—behold how
sure they are!

"These do not shun the task of unregarded
things,
Nor scorn their lot to ask alien adventurings.
For deep within them dwells the undesisting
fire
That bids their teeming cells endeavor and
aspire.

68

"Hark to the silver call of the first twilight
  thrush!
Mark where the spring lights fall with that
  faint greening flush,
And the young buds unclose on the red maple
  trees!
Have they no heart that knows?—And art
  thou less than these?"

Then as I stopped my round I marvelled at
  the sight,
For all my garden was bathed in a new light.
A glory filled the place, wherein the un-
  anxious flowers
Behold God face to face through the immortal
  hours.

PRAYERS TO THE ARCHANGELS

I

Raphael, angel of love,
Lord of the morning star,—
Splendor all proof above,
Glory beheld afar,—

Shine as thou didst of old
Through the dark Syrian night,
For seeking eyes to behold
Thy promise and portent of light.

Over our trail in the dust,
Lead through the darkness still
To the waiting world of our trust
Beyond the cross-sown hill.

Kindle our hearts with fire
As the peaks are kindled with morn,
And quicken our steps to aspire
As spring through the earth is born.

II

Gabriel, giver of knowledge,
Master of reason and thought,
Leader in ways of wisdom
For the wayward and untaught;

When through the many voices,—
The rote of the sea and the rain,
The whispering snow and the thunder,
And the ancient wind's refrain,—

The Unknown speaks to mortals
And the eager Soul gives ear,
Grant thou the understanding
That shall make the meaning clear.

Open our eyes to glory
As only a seraph can,
And teach us the angel's measure
Of the stature and freedom of man.

III

Great Michael of the flaming sword,
Unfearing, swift and strong,
Thou art the doer of the word,
The conqueror of wrong.

Of no avail were all the light
And love of Raphael,
If thou wert not at hand to smite
Traitor and infidel.

And hope would not survive the hour
Of Gabriel's "All hail!"
Save by thy pure unflinching power
To make the word prevail.

Then, Michael, give us grace to stand
Where still thy sword-flash gleams,
And love accepts thy stern command—
To win the world for dreams.

THE MESSENGERS

How shall we know the mighty ones
Who carry the Lord's commands,—
Raphael, Gabriel, Michael? Lo,
In splendor of light they come and go,
Like the rainbow with its bands.

Their robes are wrought of the color of
    flame,
Scarlet, yellow, and blue.
Raphael's yellow, pure as the sun,
That must endure while the ages run,
As love itself will do.

Gabriel's blue, as clear as a lake
That mirrors truth from its heart,
And mystical as the haze that lies
Over our mountain paradise,—
Passing the reach of art.

And Michael's scarlet, brave and glad
As the woods in early fall,
When beauty marches across the world,
And her banners of triumph are unfurled
Along our mountain wall.

So is the transport of life renewed
By the Archangels' aid,
And love and mystery and power
Are given to man with every hour,—
As it was since the worlds were made.

REVELATION

JOHN in Patmos had a vision, told in the
    Apocalypse,
Full of dark unsolved enigmas leaving rea-
    son in eclipse.

But this common world of beauty is our
    vision to behold,
As significant, entrancing, and inspired as
    John's of old.

John interpreted in fable records of the
    Hidden Mind.
Whoso reads the blessed scriptures of the
    wilderness may find

What God means by night and morning, by
    the wild bird songs in spring,
Or the mighty dirge of winter when the great
    pines sway and sing.

Whoso reads the shining legend written in
    the stony brook
By the Author of the granite and the mid-
    night's starry book,

Shall find radiant revelation. Science toils
    through glimmering night,
Until Wisdom of a sudden floods the shadowy
    peaks with light.

Wouldst thou learn God's primal secret?
    Hark what Beauty has to say,
When the spirit thrills with rapture and the
    gates of pride give way.

In the respite after seeking comes the whis-
    per of the Voice,
Bidding soul maintain her birthright,—mind
    fear not and heart rejoice.

Ask no Medium to teach thee. God exists but
    to inspire.
To the seeker comes the knowledge. To the
    kindling comes the fire.

Is thy speech as sweet as lilacs, and thy touch
    as clean as dew?
Truth is walking in the twilight still, and has
    a word for you.

Vital, vibrant, overruling are the forces of
    this earth,—
The creative urge forever bringing miracles
    to birth.

We are dream-enchanted beings, kin to
    rhythms of light and air.
Singing wind and running water have us in
    their fostering care.

Let the punctual tides instruct thee, and the
    planets give thee poise.
Take the pine tree for thy teacher whom life
    never irks nor cloys.

Live in friendship with the seasons, and their
    skill will make thee whole.
Take the bird's call and the brook's note for
    their tonic to thy soul.

Bathe in renaissance of morning, drink the
    solace twilight brings,
Feed on beauty for thy welfare and the
    strength whence rapture springs;

So thy living soul shall sense the meaning
    of the Wandering Word,
And thy being know the secret that creation's
    morning heard.

SANCTUARY

Sun fades the rosiest plaster,
Sand wears the sill away,
But the building of the Master
Must stand till Judgment Day.

The sky shall roof my chancel,
The desert be its floor,—
All lesser plans I cancel
Than these forevermore.

Its walls shall be the ranges,
Rose-ash and blue and dun,
Where the light shifts and changes—
A tapestry of the sun.

There will I have in winter
A bluebird for my choir,
And sunrise there will enter
To touch my soul with fire,

Where hoarfrost shot with morning
For the Lord's carpet lies,
With gleaming snows adorning
His walls of Paradise.

The wind among the yuccas
Will be the organ tone,
Bearing the word it utters
In music all its own.

There will I think on Beauty
Her other names to know,—
Learning the mystic duty
Of suppliants long ago.

The azure noons will teach me
The wisdom of the trail,
And the great stillness reach me
Beyond the farthest hail.

And there, his least evangel,
At sundown will I stand,
Until the Desert Angel
Shall bring me my command.

Yucca Loma Ranch,
Victorville, California.
February, 1925.

SHAMBALLAH

Have you heard of the city Shamballah,
That marvellous place in the North,
The home of the Masters of Wisdom,
Whence the Sons of the Word are sent forth?
In moments of vision we see it,
For a moment we understand,
Then it passes from sense, unsubstantial
As the shadows of gulls o'er the sand.

What Architect builded Shamballah
As frail as the wondrous new moon?
Its walls with the rose tint of morning
From no earthly quarry were hewn.
Before Him no Builder took counsel
To fashion from dust of the ground,
In beauty and order and rhythm,
A palace of color and sound.

It arose with the arches of heaven
When the planets were swung in a chime,
And those who look forth from its windows
Have watched the procession of time.
By the great Northern lights and the silence
Its inviolate portals are barred.
On cold winter nights you can see them
As they countermarch changing guard.

Have you dreamed of the mystic Shamballah,
The City under the Star,
Where the Sons of the Fire-Mist gather
And the keys of all mystery are?

When the white moon rises in splendor,
Have you said, as it lifts and gleams,
"They have lighted the Silver Lantern
In the gate of the City of Dreams."

Have you read of the fabled Shamballah
In symbols or letters of gold,
Whence issued the Bringers of Knowledge
For the saving of peoples untold?
They builded no temple save beauty,
Save truth they established no creed,
Great love was their power and purpose,
As a flower in the heart of a seed.

They heard the first flute-note in Egypt
Uplifted in longing and prayer.
When sunrise stole over the desert
To break upon Thebes, they were there.
In Babylon, Llassa, and Sarnath,
Through Galilee, Athens and Tyre
To thresholds unnamed and unnumbered
They carried the Message of Fire.

They kindled the flame unconsuming
In souls that were quick to receive,
They told of a truth that should follow
Had love but the will to believe.
From Patmos, Chaldea, and Cumae
Their servants were chosen anew,
To speak as the Logos commanded,
That the Dream of the Good might come true.

The light-bearing sons of Shamballah,
They spread the ineffable word.
And spirits who mocked it were broken,

And blessed were the spirits that heard.
The birds knew the joy of their gospel,
The windflower sprang where they trod,
And the ages were quickened to worship
Jehovah or Allah or God.

Have you heard of the speech of Shamballah,
The language that all men know
In township, pueblo, or palace,
Wherever men rest or go?
It is clear in the tones of friendship,
It is murmured in wind and rain,
It is writ in the painted desert,
And the sifting snow on the plain.

It blooms in the high Sierras,
It springs from the dust of the trail,
It flowers in golden silence
When all other speeches fail.
There is never a hint of kindness,
There is never an accent of love,
But the firmament thrills to its whisper
And the heavens are glad thereof.

Forth from that Magian City
What teachers and avatars came,
To walk through our streets in pity—
If so they might heal our shame!
From Krishna, Gautama, and Jesus
To Swedenborg, Blake, and Delsarte,
They brought us the message of brothers,
They labored and died apart.

Untold are the sons of Shamballah,
Who must carry the word without rest,
And pass, with the joy of their presence,
Like shadows of angels unguessed.
They carry no mark of their order,
No talisman men must obey.
The street of the heart is their highroad,
Their mission to lighten the way.

They came with the music of Orpheus,
With the hymns of Isaiah and Job,
With the staff and bowl of the beggar
Or the glory of Solomon's robe.
Their task from Plotinus to Browning
Was ever and never the same,—
To replenish the altars of wisdom
And guard the impalpable flame.

In this mortal fabric incarnate
What radiant souls have had birth!
The visions they cherished and quickened
Were not begotten of earth.
In music or language or color,
However their rapture was caught,
Divine were the instincts they followed,
Divine was the service they wrought.

The sweep of Beethoven and Handel
In majestical triumph or dirge,
The glories of Raphael's genius,
The splendor of Angelo's urge,
The soaring Te Deums of Gothic
Arrested in eloquent stone,—
What are these but the soul of the Ages
Immortal through color and tone!

Pure wine of the spirit they gave us,—
A gladness to make us whole,—
But we trusted to cunning to save us,
And cunning has cheated our soul.
The brand of the beast is upon us
In wantonness, folly and greed.
We have trampled the torch that should
    light us,
And our darkness is ours indeed.

The Nations are gathered to counsel,
In jealousy, envy, and fear,
Forgetting the Judgment of Karma,
And the Judgment of Karma is here.
O'er Rome, over London and Paris
The morrows of destiny wait.
Yet who now seeks word from Shamballah?
Who knocks at the Ivory Gate?

THE SPRING CALL OF WAWA

Hear the voice of Wawa in the twilight,
Now the snows are loosened on the plain!
Hear the word of Wawa going Northward,
Winging on the soft wind and the rain!
All the solemn April night resounding
With the cries of Wawa and his train.

Awake, my April children,
And hark,—that startling cry,
The wild geese going over,
A great wedge honking high!

The dark resounds with signals,
The heaven is full of wings,
And in your heart the flutter
Of wild imaginings,—

The breathless sudden impulse
To get you out of door
And hear the old goose calling
On the long trek once more.

He cries the needed warning
To steer the ragged line,
By unknown lake and river,
O'er hills of spruce and pine.

He knows the Fundy shore-line,
The dark Laurentian peaks,
And where prepared lies waiting
The feeding-ground he seeks,—

Where the first warmth of April
Is stirring in the sedge,
And the last ice is melting
Along the lake's blue edge.

Unquestioning he follows
The lead that lures him forth
For Athabascan reed-beds
And the Sunlands of the North.

Behind him press the legions,
The drive that must prevail;
Before him lie the wonder,
The whisper and the trail.

He may not doubt nor falter,
He may not quit nor tire
Who leads the lusty migrants
To the waters of desire.

O you who hear the music
Within the April rain,
And send your hearts to journey
With Wawa and his train,

You too shall learn the magic
That makes the woodlands ring,—
The mystery that fashions
The beauty of the spring.

In sugar bush and orchard
The sap is sweet and strong,
And meadow lot and clearing
Are waiting for their song.

Then with the quickened joyance
Lift up your hearts on high,
To the gospel of enchantment
Announced along the sky.

You truly shall inherit
The land of Wawa's dream,
And Wawa's God shall lead you
Beside his silver stream.

Then fear no more, you faithful
Who in the Earthland dwell.
Hark to the old goose honking,
'Tis Spring and all is well!

Hear the voice of Wawa in the midnight
O'er the stirring land that lies below!
Hear the word of Wawa on the long trail
Where the hidden wisdom bids him go!
Get you to the wilds again with Wawa,—
Who can tell what secrets you shall know!